discovermore

Space Science

Exploring Objects in the Sky

Elizabeth Pruet

Britannica Educational Publishing

IN ASSOCIATION WITH

THE ROSEN PUBLISHING GROUP

Published in 2026 by Britannica Educational Publishing (a trademark of Encyclopædia Britannica, Inc.) in association with The Rosen Publishing Group, Inc.
2544 Clinton Street, Buffalo, NY 14224

Distributed exclusively by Rosen Publishing.
To see additional Britannica Educational Publishing titles, go to rosenpublishing.com.

Editor: Danielle Haynes
Book Design: Michael Flynn

Photo Credits: Cover Nihit RPG/Shutterstock.com; (series background) Dai Yim/Shutterstock.com; p. 4 Denis Belitsky/Shutterstock.com; p. 5 NicoElNino/Shutterstock.com; p. 6 BlueRingMedia/Shutterstock.com; p. 7 muratart/Shutterstock.com; pp. 8, 17 (top), 19 (main), 20, 22 courtesy of NASA; p. 9 Ben G151/Shutterstock.com; p. 10 Laura Hedien/Shutterstock.com; p. 11 Designua/Shutterstock.com; p. 13 (top) Jan Garbers/Shutterstock.com; p. 13 (bottom) aeonWAVE/Shutterstock.com; p. 15 (top) George Trumpeter/Shutterstock.com; p. 15 (bottom) Designua/Shutterstock.com; p. 17 (bottom) Sudakarn Vivatvanichkul/Shutterstock.com; p. 19 (inset) https://commons.wikimedia.org/wiki/File:JWST_Full_Mirror.jpg; p. 21 (left) https://commons.wikimedia.org/wiki/File:Iridium_satellite_replica.jpg; p. 21 (right) https://commons.wikimedia.org/wiki/File:Strela-2M.jpg; p. 23 EHT Collaboration; p. 24 (top) Denis Belitsky/Shutterstock.com; p. 24 (bottom) Designua/Shutterstock.com; p. 26 Smit/Shutterstock.com; p. 27 WooHoo Production/Shutterstock.com; p. 28 AstroStar/Shutterstock.com; p. 29 Frame Stock Footage/Shutterstock.com.

Cataloging-in-Publication Data
Names: Pruet, Elizabeth.
Title: Exploring objects in the sky / Elizabeth Pruet.
Description: New York : Britannica Educational Publishing, in association with Rosen Educational Services, 2026. | Series: Discover more: space science | Includes glossary and index.
Identifiers: ISBN 9781641905398 (library bound) | ISBN 9781641905381 (pbk) | ISBN 9781641905404 (ebook)
Subjects: LCSH: Stars--Juvenile literature. | Planets--Juvenile literature. | Solar system--Juvenile literature. | Astronomy--Juvenile literature.
Classification: LCC QB801.7 P78 2026 | DDC 523--dc23

Manufactured in the United States of America

Some of the images in this book illustrate individuals who are models. The depictions do not imply actual situations or events.

CPSIA Compliance Information: Batch #CWBRIT26. For further information contact Rosen Publishing at 1-800-237-9932.

Contents

Looking Up

Since ancient times, people have looked up into the sky and tried to explain the things they see there. Different cultures have seen different patterns in the stars. They have named constellations after familiar animals, everyday objects, and story characters. Ancient peoples also believed that angry gods threw lightning bolts from the heavens to punish humans on Earth. Since these times, scientists have learned much about what is really in the sky.

For thousands of years, people have found patterns in the stars called constellations.

Some of the lights we see in the night sky might look like stars, but they're really human-made satellites.

When people think of objects in the sky, they may think about planets, the sun, the moon, and the constellations. Many other bodies orbit Earth and the sun, however. Some of these bodies are natural. Others are human made. The sky in Earth's **atmosphere** holds many interesting objects as well. We may not need a telescope to see them, but they are no less dazzling. These objects in the skies have brought wonder, awe, and fear to humans as long as we've existed on Earth.

WORD WISE

THE ATMOSPHERE IS THE LAYER OF GAS THAT SURROUNDS EARTH.

Shining Stars

Stars look to us like little points of light, but they're really huge glowing balls of gases. They are grouped into galaxies. The Milky Way galaxy alone contains hundreds of billions of stars. Most stars are incredibly far away.

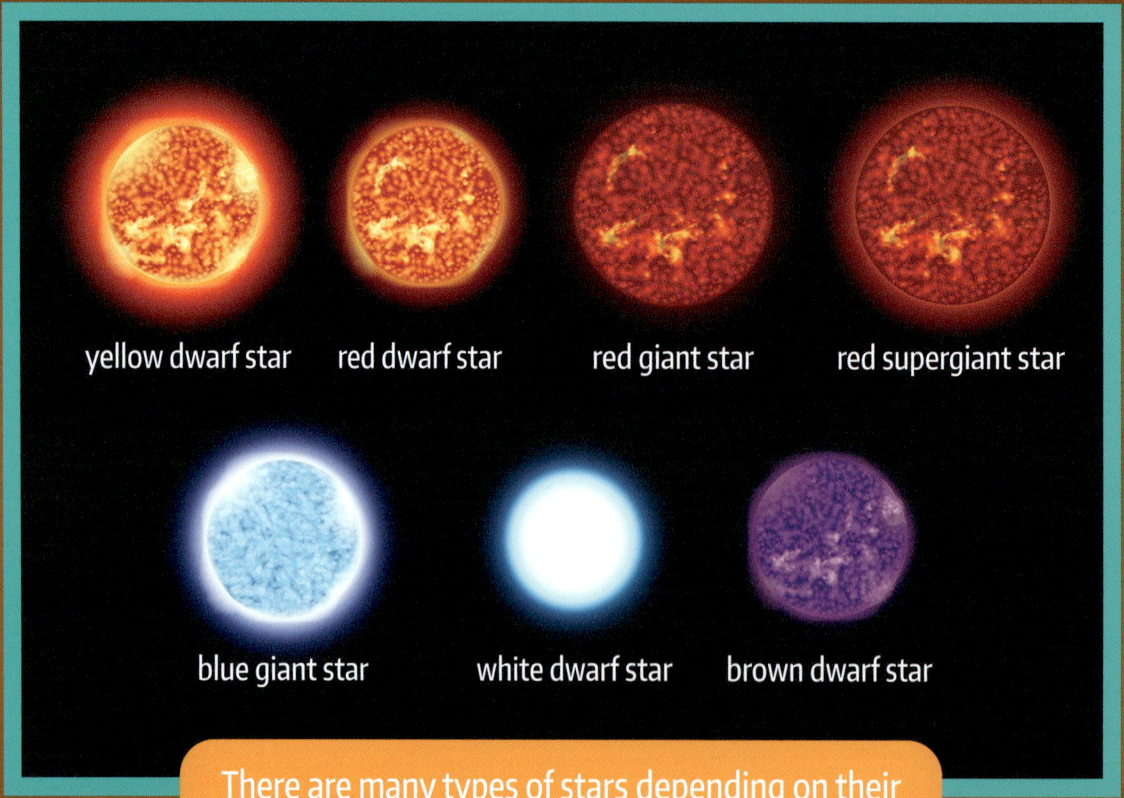

There are many types of stars depending on their size and temperature. Our sun is a yellow dwarf.

The large, bright light near the center of this galaxy is an exploding star called a supernova.

Nearly all stars are mostly made up of a gas called hydrogen. A star's core is very hot. Great pressure squeezes the core, causing some of the hydrogen to change into another gas, helium. This makes the star shine.

Stars may be different in size, temperature, brightness, and color. After shining for billions of years, a star uses up all its hydrogen. Small and medium stars slowly cool down and stop shining. Large stars end with an explosion called a supernova. Some stars collapse into a black hole, while others may become a nebula.

Consider This

The sun is a star. Its size and brightness are average. What does this mean for the sun's future?

Gigantic Galaxies

The planet Earth is part of a galaxy, a group of stars, clouds of gas, and dust particles that move together through the universe. There are billions of galaxies in the universe. They probably formed billions of years ago, soon after the universe began.

The smaller galaxies are made up of millions of stars. The largest galaxies contain trillions of stars.

There are more than 100 galaxies in this NASA image using a telescope, and each has up to trillions of stars.

In really dark places on Earth, you can see arms of the Milky Way sweep across the night sky.

The sun, Earth, and other planets of the solar system are part of the Milky Way galaxy. Most galaxies move through the universe as part of clusters, or groups, of galaxies. The Milky Way is at one end of a cluster called the Local Group. It includes more than 40 galaxies. The most common type of galaxy is a **spiral galaxy**, which is shaped like a pinwheel with bands or arms.

WORD WISE

SPIRAL GALAXIES ARE SHAPED LIKE PINWHEELS. ELLIPTICAL GALAXIES CAN LOOK LIKE A FOOTBALL. IRREGULAR GALAXIES ARE UNUSUALLY SHAPED.

Lightning and Thunder

One of the brightest and loudest things to see in our sky is lightning. Lightning is electricity released from Earth's atmosphere during thunderstorms. Water droplets inside a cloud carry positive and negative electrical charges. Lightning occurs when too many negative charges build up in a cloud. To balance these negative charges, positive charges form on the ground. Because opposite charges attract, the negative charges in the cloud want to join the positive charges on the ground.

While beautiful, lightning can be dangerous to humans, so stay indoors when you see these flashes in the sky.

How Lightning Is Formed

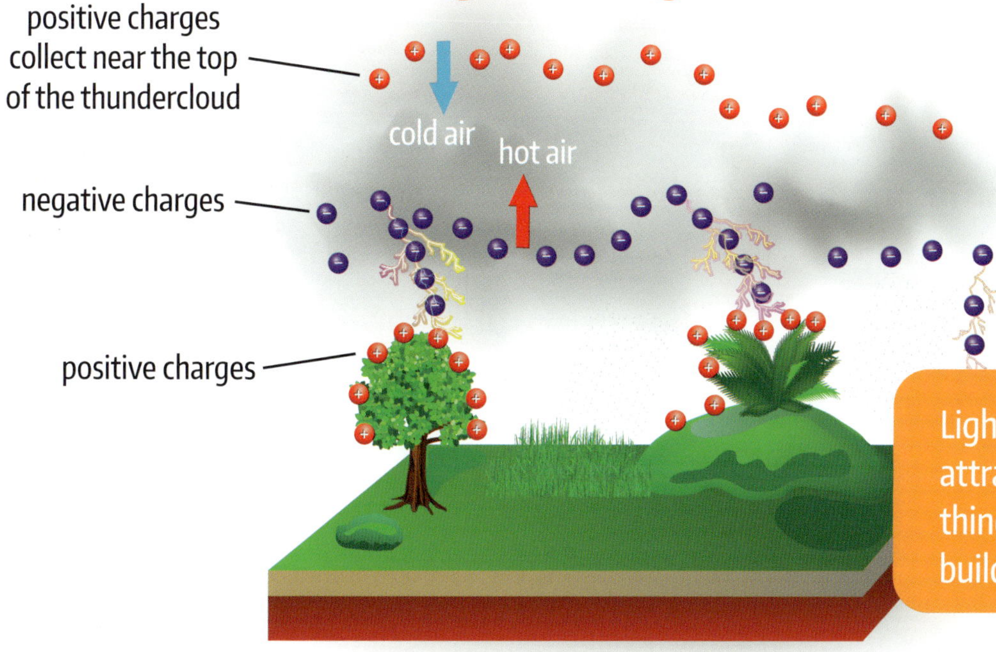

Lightning is attracted to tall things, such as buildings and trees.

Eventually the cloud releases a strong, negatively charged electrical current. As the negative current heads toward the ground, a positively charged current jumps from the ground to meet it. When the currents join, they create a bright flash of lightning, followed by **thunder**. The more closely the thunder follows a bolt of lightning, the closer the lightning is to you.

WORD WISE

THE LOUD BOOM THAT FOLLOWS LIGHTNING IS CALLED THUNDER. WHEN ELECTRICITY FROM LIGHTNING HEATS AND EXPANDS GASES IN THE AIR, THEY MAKE A LOUD NOISE.

Moving Meteoroids

What we often call a shooting star is usually a meteoroid. This is a chunk of rock or metal from space that falls through Earth's atmosphere. Most meteoroids burn up in the atmosphere. This creates a bright streak of light called a meteor. Meteors are also called shooting stars. If a meteoroid survives its fall and reaches Earth's surface, it is called a meteorite.

Almost all meteoroids are formed from material that breaks off objects in space called comets or asteroids. The chunk of rock or metal may enter Earth's atmosphere traveling as fast as 45 miles (72 km) per second. Most meteoroids melt from the heat or break up from the pressure within seconds of entering Earth's atmosphere. Scientists think a large meteorite hitting Earth is what caused the dinosaurs to die out.

Meteor showers happen when Earth passes through a trail of rocks from a comet or asteroid.

compare and contrast

Meteors, meteoroids, and meteorites all sound very similar. Compare and contrast the three objects.

A large meteorite hit Australia about 300,000 years ago, leaving this huge crater. Wolfe Creek Meteorite Crater is about 2,871 feet (875 m) across.

Icy Comets

Some meteoroids come from comets. A comet is a small chunk of ice and dust that orbits the sun. It is sometimes described as a "dirty snowball."

Most comets travel very far into the solar system. It can take from several years to many thousands of years to complete one orbit. The best-known comet is Halley's Comet. It can be seen from Earth about every 76 years.

The main part of a comet is called the nucleus. It is made of frozen water and gases plus dust and rock. When the comet gets close to the sun, a cloud of gas and dust builds up around the comet. Eventually energy and particles from the sun push some of the gas and dust out to form tails. Sometimes, some of the pieces of rock that break off a comet make their way to Earth's atmosphere and become a meteor.

People on Earth could see a comet called NEOWISE without the use of telescopes in 2020.

compare and contrast

A comet's orbit is shaped like a long oval. Compare and contrast comet orbits to those of planets.

The cloud of gas and dust that builds up around a comet as it nears the sun is called the coma.

Dwarf Planets

There are eight planets in our solar system, but there are several more considered dwarf planets. Dwarf planets are small planets, and like the eight main planets of the solar system, they orbit the sun. The difference is that planets are large enough to affect the smaller bodies nearby. Planets are big enough to either push these bodies away or sweep them up. Dwarf planets are not big enough to do this.

Until recently, there was no way to classify dwarf planets. In 2006, the International Astronomical Union (IAU) decided that Pluto was not a planet. Pluto had been considered the ninth planet of the solar system. Its category was changed to dwarf planet. Eris, Ceres, Makemake, and Haumea are other dwarf planets in our solar system. The IAU believes there could be more than 100 other dwarf planets in our solar system.

Scientists got their closest look at Pluto in 2015 when the New Horizons spacecraft came within 476,000 miles (768 km) of its surface.

compare and contrast

Dwarf planets are smaller than the planet Mercury. Look up the diameters of dwarf planets and compare and contrast them to the other planets.

This illustration of the dwarf planet Haumea shows its unusual shape. It's shaped like a football because it has such a fast spin, making one rotation in four hours.

Human-Made Satellites

The word "satellite" might make you think of metal objects floating around Earth, beaming signals and taking photos. But a satellite is any object that orbits a larger object in space. Satellites can be natural or artificial (made by people). Artificial satellites are sent into space to gather information. Most are launched into space by rockets.

Artificial satellites have many purposes. Humans live briefly on **space stations** to collect information about space. The Hubble Space Telescope is a scientific satellite that orbits Earth. It sees the sky more clearly than telescopes on the ground. Communications satellites help send telephone calls, radio and television programs, and computer information all over the world. Airplanes, ships, and cars with special equipment can use information from satellites to find their way from place to place. Military forces use satellites for spying. Satellites are also used to study the weather and for getting internet signals to remote locations on Earth.

One of NASA's newest artificial satellites is the James Webb Space Telescope. It orbits far away from Earth and takes photos of distant objects, such as the Cat's Paw Nebula, seen here.

WORD WISE

A SPACE STATION IS A SPECIAL KIND OF SATELLITE USED BY ASTRONAUTS. ASTRONAUTS CAN LIVE ON A SPACE STATION FOR MONTHS WHILE THEY GATHER INFORMATION AND PERFORM EXPERIMENTS.

Junk in Space

There's trash orbiting all around Earth. We call this space junk. This junk travels at speeds up to 17,500 miles (28,000 km) per hour. These speeds are fast enough for debris to cause damage. Even a chip of paint from an abandoned space station can harm a spacecraft.

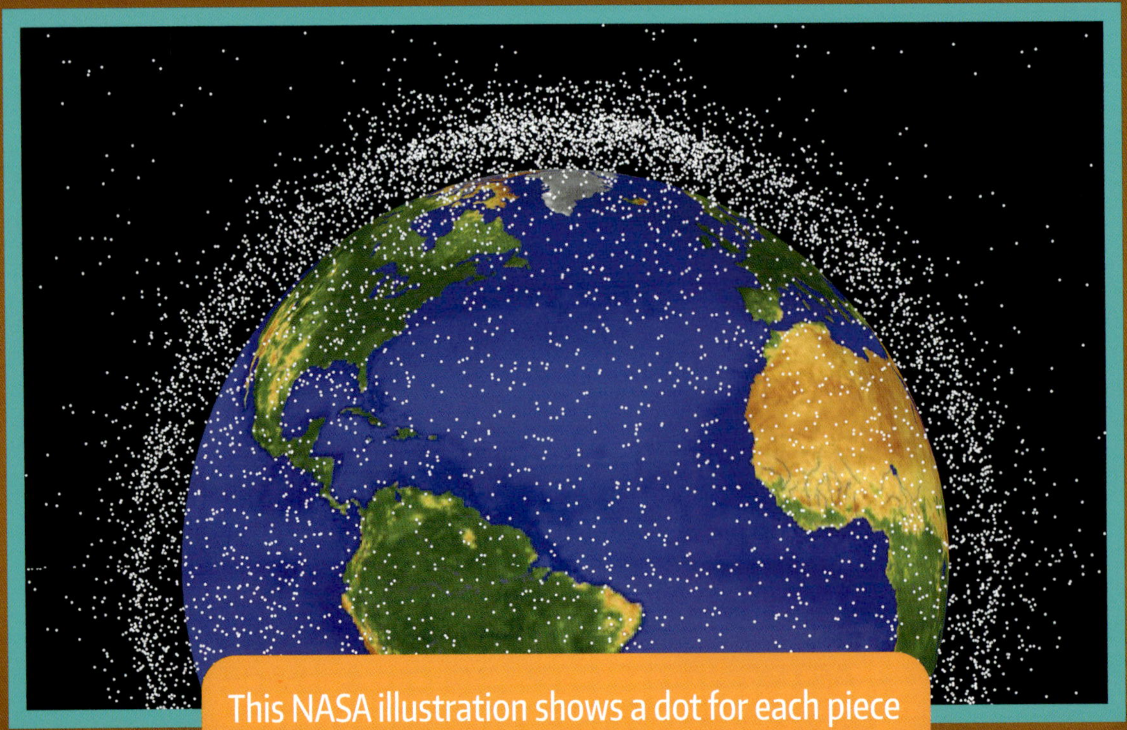

This NASA illustration shows a dot for each piece of space debris orbiting close to Earth.

In 2009, the U.S. satellite Iridium 33 (left) and the Russian military satellite Kosmos 2251 accidentally crashed into each other in space, creating more than 1,000 pieces of space junk.

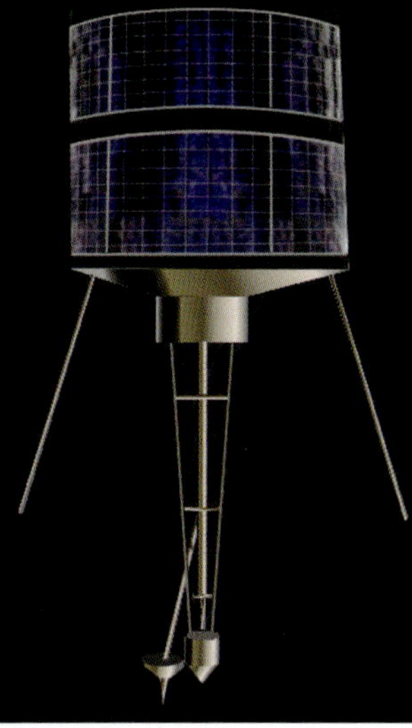

Space junk particles can be artificial or natural. Meteoroids are an example of natural debris. They orbit the sun. Artificial debris can be anything that no longer works, such as old satellites or abandoned launches.

The U.S. military uses radar and telescopes to keep track of any space debris larger than a softball. If NASA thinks there's a danger to astronauts, it plans a course of action for spacecraft to avoid the debris. It would be expensive to try to clean up the nearly 6,000 tons (5,443 metric tons) of space junk in low Earth orbit.

Consider This

Running into space junk can cause the scattering of even more debris. How can such accidents be avoided?

Mysterious Black Holes

Not all objects in the sky can be seen easily. A black hole is an area in space with an especially strong force called gravity. This gravity pulls in everything that gets close. Nothing, not even light, can escape from a black hole once it has been pulled in.

Black holes are not actually holes. They have great amounts of material packed in very tightly. They are called "black" because they are invisible to the naked eye.

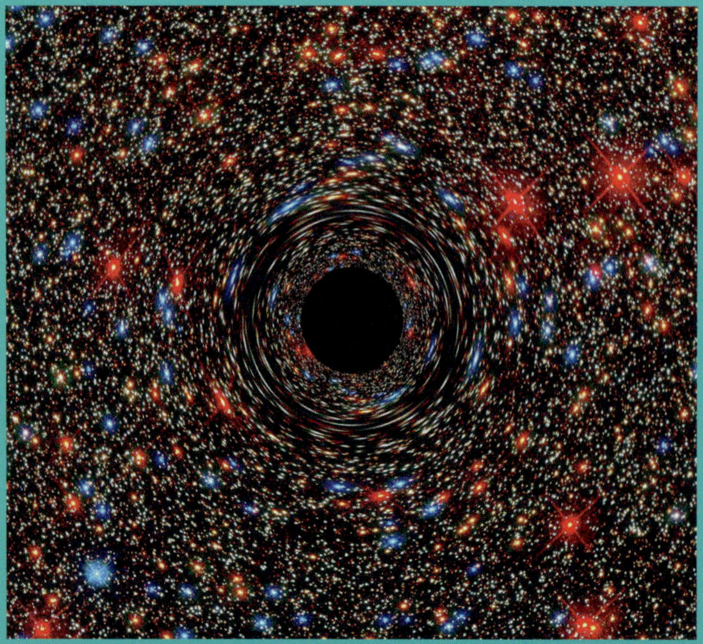

The gravity of a black hole is so strong, it distorts, or bends, space around it, as is shown in the blurry stars near the center in this illustration.

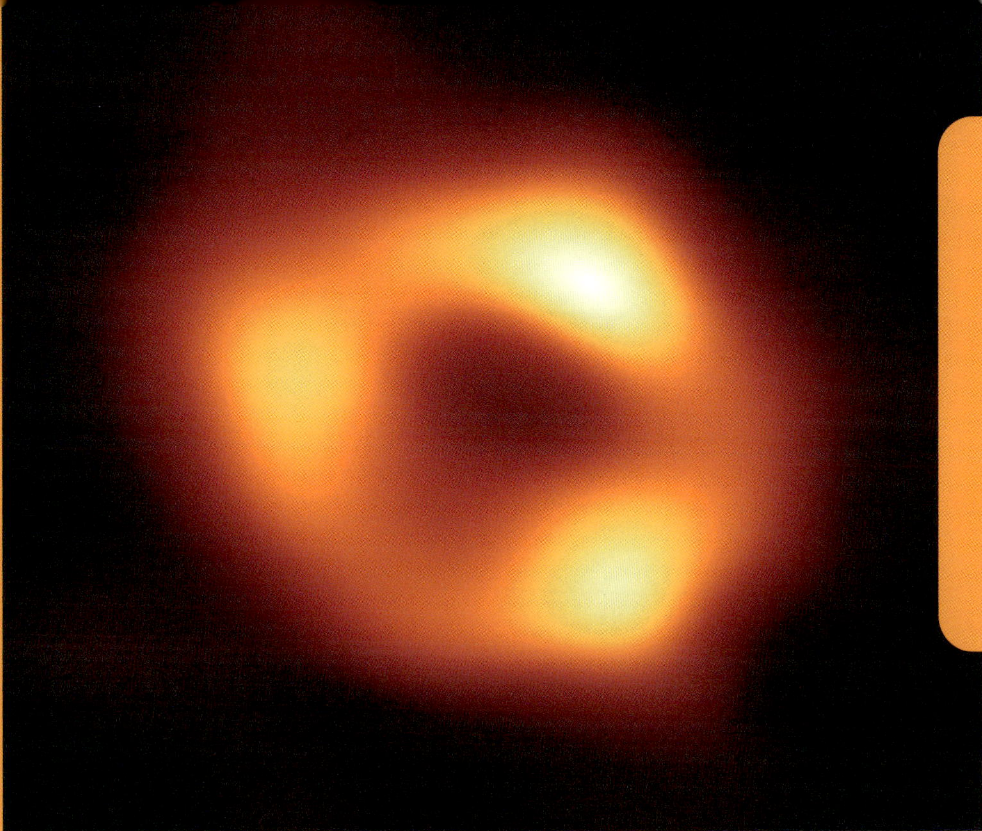

Scientists took the first image of the supermassive black hole at the center of the Milky Way in 2022. It's called Sagittarius A* because it's near that constellation from Earth's view.

A black hole can be formed when a huge star uses up its fuel. When a star runs out of its fuel, it can't counter the gravity that pulls the star in on itself. The gravity crushes the star smaller and smaller, and it becomes a black hole. There are several types of black holes, including supermassive black holes.

Consider This

Only stars that are more than three times as large as the sun become black holes. Are black holes heavy or light?

Awesome Auroras

A little closer to home, auroras are dazzling displays of colored light that sometimes appear in the night sky. They occur in Earth's far northern and far southern regions. In the Northern Hemisphere such a display is known as aurora borealis, or the northern lights. In the Southern Hemisphere it is called aurora australis, or the southern lights. Auroras are named after Aurora, the ancient Roman goddess of the dawn.

Auroras take many shapes and forms, with arcs and rays of colored light being the most common. The light may look like shimmering curtains, bands, waves, or clouds. An aurora constantly changes shape as the light moves across the sky. The light may also alternately brighten and fade. Auroras are stronger and brighter when the sun gives off large solar flares, which affect Earth's magnetic field.

Auroras are most easily seen close to the North and South Poles, but sometimes they're bigger and can be seen in other areas.

compare and contrast

Auroras are caused by the sun. Compare and contrast auroras with lightning, which is electricity released during thunderstorms.

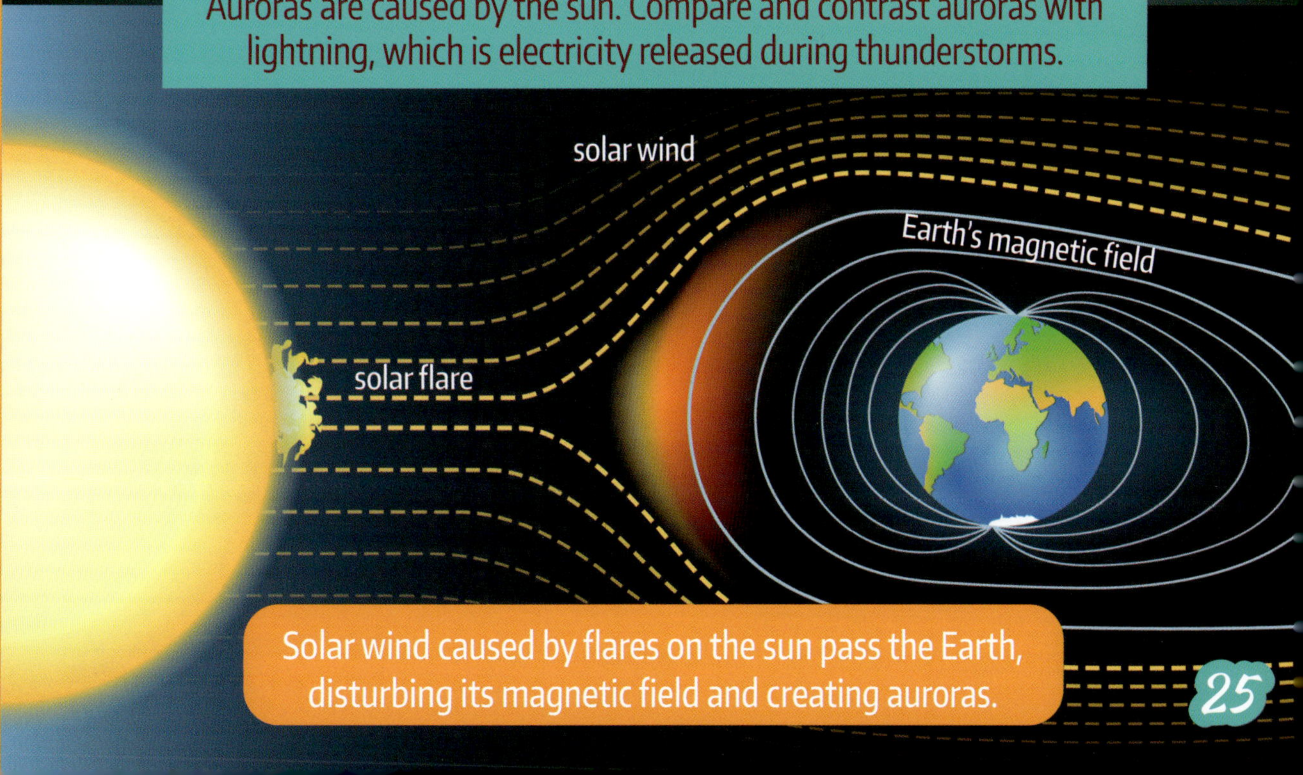

Solar wind caused by flares on the sun pass the Earth, disturbing its magnetic field and creating auroras.

Colors of the Rainbow

One of the most beautiful things you might see in the sky is a rainbow. A rainbow is a multicolored arc, or curved line, in the sky. Rainbows form when the sun's rays strike raindrops falling from faraway clouds. Rainbows appear in the part of the sky opposite the sun, usually in the early morning or late afternoon. From inside to outside, the colors of a **primary rainbow** are violet, indigo, blue, green, yellow, orange, and red.

Rainbows appear in the sky after rain as the sun comes back out.

Have you ever noticed a rainbow inside your home? Just like raindrops, glass can sometimes act as a prism, separating the colors of light.

Sunlight travels through space in the form of waves. Light waves with different wavelengths appear as different colors. Usually, all light waves blend to form white light. But when light waves pass through raindrops, they separate. The separated light waves appear as the colors of a rainbow. In this way, the raindrop acts as a prism.

WORD WISE

A PRIMARY BOW IS THE BRIGHTEST AND MOST COMMON TYPE OF RAINBOW. A DOUBLE RAINBOW IS CALLED A SECONDARY BOW.

Looking to the Future

For thousands of years, people had stories and myths to explain stars in the sky and other happenings. Advances in science have changed that. Thanks to advances in astronomy—the study of all objects outside Earth's atmosphere—we know why the sun appears to rise each morning. We understand where lightning comes from.

Some Earth-based telescopes are so big, special buildings called observatories must be built for them.

While we might think of astronomers as working at telescopes, many use computers to look at images from space-based telescopes.

Strong cameras and telescopes allow astronomers to observe distant objects. The Hubble and James Webb Space Telescopes orbit around Earth as floating observatories. They magnify and record images of distant space objects. They then send the information to astronomers on Earth. Other spacecraft also have gathered information about the sun, moon, and planets. For as much as we know, however, space still contains mysteries. Scientists are still inventing new tools to look farther and deeper.

Consider This

Before calendars and clocks, people looked to the sun and the stars. How do you think they used objects in the sky to keep track of time?

Glossary

abandoned Something left behind.

astronomer A scientist who studies space.

collapse To fall or shrink in on oneself.

core The center part of something.

culture The beliefs and ways of life of a certain group of people.

debris The remains of something broken or destroyed.

expand To become bigger.

launch To send something, often into the sky or space.

nebula A cloud of gas or dust in space.

orbit The path taken by one body circling around another body.

particle A small part of something; a basic unit of matter.

pressure A force acting against an opposing force.

radar A system used to detect objects.

rotation The process of turning in a circle.

supernova The explosion of a very large star.

telescope An instrument used to see objects in outer space.

universe Everything that exists on Earth and in space.

For More Information

Books

Lombardo, Jennifer, and Kristen Rajczak Nelson. *Rainbows*. Buffalo, NY: Scientific American Educational Publishing, 2025.

Poppele, Jonathan. *Stargazing for Kids: An Introduction to Astronomy*. Cambridge, MN: Adventure Publications, 2022.

Williams, Ann. *Supernovas and More Sizzling Sights*. Minneapolis, MN: A&D Xtreme, 2025.

Websites

NASA: Space Place
www.spaceplace.nasa.gov
Visit the official NASA website dedicated specifically to young readers, and learn more about objects in the night sky.

National Weather Service: Just for Kids
www.weather.gov/cae/justforkids.html
Read more about weather to learn about the objects you see in the sky a little closer to home.

Index